BEING AWAY FROM YOUR PARENTS

by Joy Berry • Illustrated by Maggie Smith

SCHOLASTIC INC.

New York   Toronto   London   Auckland   Sydney
Mexico City   New Delhi   Hong Kong   Buenos Aires

ISBN 0-439-34163-9

10 9 8 7 6 5 4 3 2 1   02 03 04 05 06
Printed in the U.S.A.
First printing, June 2002

Hello, my name is Henrietta.
I live with Nate.

Nate goes a lot of places
with his parents.

Like Nate, you probably like going places with your parents.

But sometimes you need to go places without them.

And sometimes they need to go places without you.

Sometimes one or both of your parents need to run errands without you.

Sometimes you like to have time alone with your friends.

And sometimes your parents need and want to spend time with other adults.

When you are away from your parents, you might feel uncertain about things.

You might worry that they won't come back or that they'll be gone for a long time.

And you might wonder if your baby-sitter will take care of you the way your parents do.

Try not to worry when you are away from your parents.

Remember that they will come back.

Also remember that there will be a responsible person to take care of you while they're away.

That person might not do things exactly like your parents.

But doing things a little differently can be fun.

When you think about your parents going away, you might feel like you don't have a say about what's happening.

You might wonder why they are leaving or why you can't go with them.

You might wish you could make decisions about their going away.

When your parents are planning a trip, talk to them about how you feel.

Ask them where they are going and how long they will be gone.

Write down the phone number where they can be reached.

You might not be able to keep your parents from going away.

But you can help plan fun things to do while they're gone.

When your parents are away, you might feel left out.

You might wonder if they'll do fun and exciting things that you won't get to do.

Try not to feel left out when your parents are away.

Remember that children can't always do the things grown-ups do.

Besides, many adult activities aren't fun for children.

When your parents are away, you might be upset because you couldn't go with them.

You might be upset because you wish you were getting your way.

It helps to remember that nobody gets what they want all the time.

When your parents are away, you might feel sad and lonely.

It might help to talk about how you feel.

All children and parents have to be away from each other sometimes.

But after they've been away, being together is even more special!

Let's talk about . . . **Joy Berry!**

As the inventor of self-help books for kids, Joy Berry has written over 250 books that teach children about taking responsibility for themselves and their actions. With sales of over 80 million copies, Joy's books have helped millions of parents and their kids.

Through interesting stories that kids can relate to, Joy Berry's Let's Talk About books explain how to handle even the toughest situations and emotions. Written in a clear, simple style and illustrated with bright, humorous pictures, the Let's Talk About books are fun, informative, and they really work!

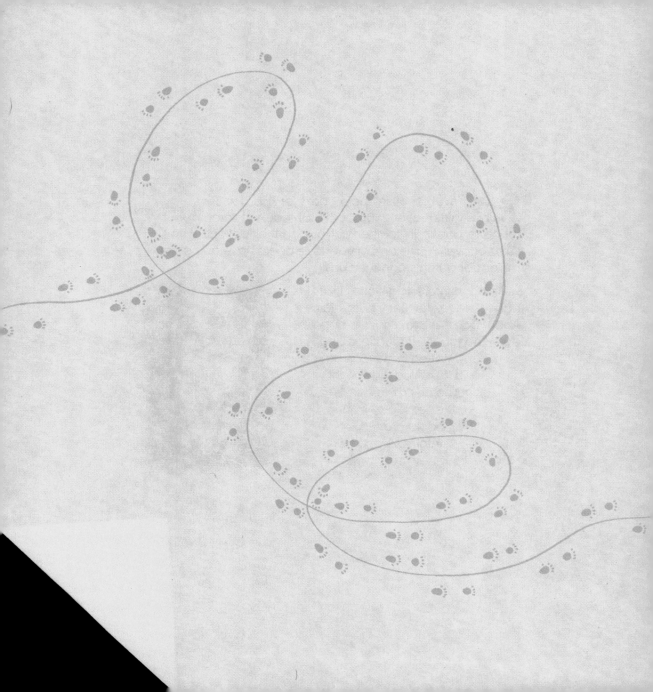